HOW TO MANAGE DIFFICULT PEOPLE

J ROCHIE HOLOHAN

Executive Coach & Training Consultant

ISBN - 10: 1482025086
ISBN - 13: 9781482025088

Please help us …

… to help them …

All the revenues from these books are shared with <u>Cuan Counselling</u>, a non-profit charity based in Dingle in County Kerry in Ireland. They offer a (free-of-charge) local support and counselling service to people, especially young males, who are at risk of self harm or suicide.

So, … we are really hoping that you will recommend this book to your Friends and Colleagues, … however, we ask you to please <u>not</u> photocopy it, circulate it or pass it along. Do please invite them to buy or download a copy of their own from Amazon, … thank you! Of course, you can also send it as a gift from the Amazon website to a Friend or Colleague, … when you have read it, you just might!

<u>GUARANTEE</u>: If you buy or download a copy for yourself and if you take the thirty or so minutes to read it … and you are not satisfied that you have got full value for your 'buck', … Rochie will buy the coffees, when next ye meet!

Take a break ...

Take a 'time out' for thirty
minutes to read this book,
... it could prove to be one of
your best investments ever!

*Business
Leader &
Chamber
President,*

Pat Owens.

"Rochie had to push me hard to get me to read the first four-page article he gave me ... detailed reading would not be my style. As soon as I read it, it was like being suddenly struck by lightning. I knew immediately that those twenty minutes would become the best business investment I had ever made. After forty years, I had totally changed my approach to business in twenty minutes.

I then went on to join my first two-day workshop with Rochie, when I made another very definite business decision - from then on, I would join Rochie annually in one of his workshops, ... just for me! Since then, I have tirelessly recommended his coaching workshops to my business colleagues.

I strongly recommend that you take the thirty or so minutes to read this book, ... it could well be one of the best investments you will ever make."

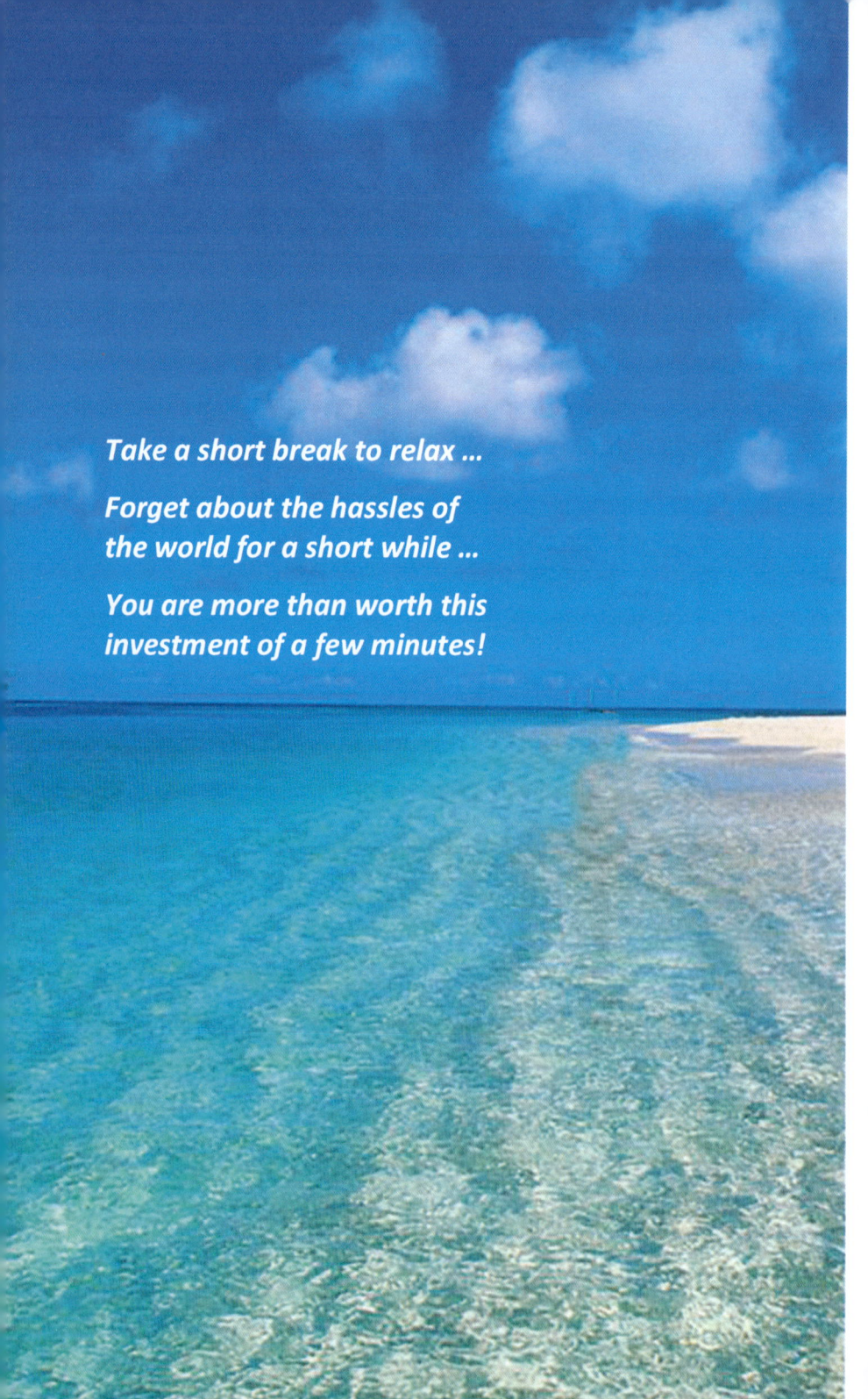

Take a short break to relax ...

Forget about the hassles of the world for a short while ...

You are more than worth this investment of a few minutes!

CONTENTS

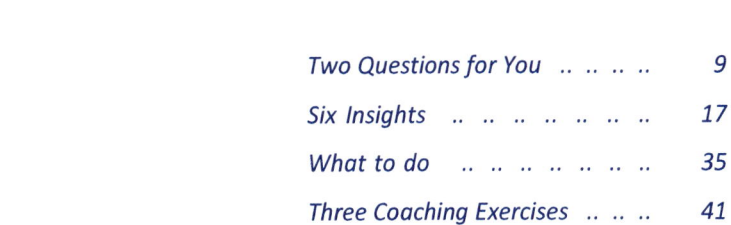

For this short break,

PLEASE RESET YOUR WATCH TO ME TIME ...

Hi, here's a question for you:

What usually drives you crazy?
What keeps you awake at night?

Day in, day out, what gets 'up your nose' when you are at work, when you are out socialising with your friends, when you are on holiday or when you are at home?

When I ask the Participants in our coaching workshops about their current hassles at work, they can so easily talk about such

items as ... the ever-increasing pressures on them; the ever-higher customer demands; the budget demands; the soaring costs; the endless meetings; the incessant demands for excessive reports from the ever-growing bureaucratic monster; the constant interruptions; the steady stream of callers and visitors; the non-stop e-mails and phone calls, ...

<u>If I asked you about your current hassles at work (and in your life), what would you talk about?</u>

The Participants in our coaching workshops can and do talk about everything and anything, except:

If we are totally honest with ourselves, is it not true that, more than all of those items above, it can be the hassle of dealing with 'difficult people' at work that can largely determine how manageable or how stressful we find our work lives, ... and our lives in general?

As it happens, we often continue on with our conversations in those coaching workshops about our people problems. To my amazement, some Participants report that, in their experience, there is nothing quite as stressful as having a dysfunctional poor performer working and reporting to them, ... some tell me that it is even more painful than working and reporting to a dysfunctional boss, ... could you believe that?

In frank moments, many Participants tell me they feel intense anger and hurt with what some people say and do at work, when they are out socialising, when they are at home or even when they are with their own family.

In fact, when they take the time to stop and really think about it, … so many Participants report that they feel that their own lives are being made quite miserable by the few 'difficult people' in their circle, … these 'difficult people' hammer their self-esteem and make them feel annoyed and down, … daily, … sometimes many times a day!

These 'difficult people', they say, can show zero respect for them, judge them, criticise them, put them down, try to control them, try to provoke them, ignore them, refuse to listen to them, … or even ridicule or mock them or what they say or believe. All of these can cause so much of that anger and hurt.

Angela, a Participant in a recent coaching workshop, had this to say: "Usually, I have an easy confident style at work, … but when a particular difficult co-worker starts, I feel I can do nothing right."

SOME PARTICIPANTS REPORT THAT THESE 'DIFFICULT PEOPLE' CAN BEHAVE IN REALLY OUTRAGEOUS WAYS TOWARDS THEM.

As a coach and trainer, I am often amazed and shocked at just how many Participants, who have managed to build for themselves such great lives, ... and, yet, they continue to allow these 'difficult people' in their circle to virtually ruin it all for them.

Stress can be defined as the inner psychological damage caused by the suppression of the urge to choke the living crap out of some plonker, who really deserves it ...

Ah, ... just a joke!

<u>Why do you think they allow this to happen so often? Do you allow it to happen to you?</u>

Not so long ago, it was quite usual for authors and Business & Life Coaches to go as far as saying that the quality of our lives can be directly co-related to the quality of our relationships.

Another question for you:

How do you usually respond or react to the 'taunts' of the 'difficult people' in your circle?

Too often, Participants tell me that their reaction to those 'attacks' of the 'difficult people' is to instantly become agitated themselves and to attack back, trying to be just as aggressive in return, giving back what they got and better, … they are drawn into playing the 'difficult people' at their own game. Or alternatively, their reaction is to say nothing and go extremely quiet and sulk, full of self-pity, yet seething with rage and resentment, … dreaming of revenge but, in truth, they just decide to avoid them, if that is possible .

Also, fear is often mentioned as being a factor in our typical response, whether that be 'loud' or 'silent'. That fear can be about being made to feel even smaller or about being made to look even smaller, … perhaps in front of our friends, work colleagues or family members.   Some Participants describe a sensation of being paralysed or frozen by fear during the 'attacks' of 'difficult people'.

How do you usually react to their attitudes, their behaviours, what they say and their horrible taunts?

How can we not know that any defence such as those will make little difference to how we feel? And, of course, such will do nothing at all to rectify the problem or to change things, all of which may well repeat themselves over and over again, ... what a way to live!

It may be that, when we react or respond in those ways, we are just not thinking. Or, perhaps, our hope is to avoid or lessen or undo those feelings of anger, failure, hurt, being put down, lowered self-esteem or rejection.

Strangely, all the Participants say that, in some way, they know intuitively deep-down that their own reaction to the provocation of 'difficult people' is part of the disastrous game, that is played out again and again ... part of the problem!

Another Participant in a coaching workshop, Mark, explained: "I know all that for sure. I know that it is not very intelligent of me to allow myself to be provoked into 'flying off the handle', but in the heat of the moment, it just happens to me, ... I blurt out my angry response, before I really realise what is going on."

So many of the Participants nodded their understanding.

In order to better manage the 'difficult people' in our lives, there are six basic insights of critical value, which I would like to share with you.

It will come as no surprise to you to hear that the main hope of this book is to get you to stop and to review your thinking about and your responses to the 'difficult people' in your life, ... to allow you to change your thinking, your feelings, your behaviour and your whole approach to managing these 'difficult people', ... should you really wish that!

A most useful quote from Marianne Williamson is this: "You must learn a new way to think, before you can master a new way to be."

We must build that new (or re-newed) thinking, in order to better manage the 'difficult people' in our circle. The Participants in our coaching workshops consistently report that these six basic insights are the most useful to them in their journey to better managing the 'difficult people' in their lives. Enjoy, ...

INSIGHT NO 1 ...

... THE OUTSIDE STORY

The one insight of single greatest value in interacting and communicating with 'difficult people' is this: What any other person believes, thinks, feels, says or does is about them, ... it is 100% about them, ... it is not about you.

> *What any other person believes, thinks, feels, says or does is 100% about them ...*
>
> *It is not about you!*

What they say or do reflects where they are at in their lives at the minute - their mood today; the side of the bed they got out of; their prejudices; how they are coping with their stresses; their self-perceptions; their current self-esteem; ... really, how they now feel about themselves; ...

It is outside of you, out there, their problem, ...

IT IS ABSOLUTELY SO CRITICAL THAT YOU LEARN THIS HABIT OF <u>NOT INTERNALISING ANY OF THAT OUTSIDE STUFF!</u>

All the great leaders and public speakers, and all the excellent negotiators, that I have known or studied, ... they all had mastered this ability to distinguish between what goes on outside their skin from what goes on inside. They do not let the negativity through, they do not let it impact on them ... not on their inner workings; not on their inner thoughts nor feelings.

Certainly, they would never, ever allow outside stuff to decide their decisions, words or actions. What goes on outside does not unduly concern them, ... not really their business!

It is critical that you too come to realise this more and more. When 'difficult people' hit on you, you will now know to stop and ask yourself: "What is this saying about him or her?" You will now know that it is out there, outside of you, nothing about you, ... not really your business at all.

Here is a very short story for you:

It is a story much loved by Business & Life Coaches to illustrate this first insight, … it is based directly on John Powell's 1975 book, "Why am I afraid to tell you who I am?"

John tells the story of accompanying a Friend one morning to the local news-stand for a newspaper.

His Friend greeted the local newsman with great courtesy, in return he received gruff and discourteous service. As the newspaper was shoved rudely in his direction, his Friend politely smiled and wished the newsman a nice week-end.

Walking back the street, John asked: "Does he always treat you so rudely?" "Yes, unfortunately he does." "And are you always so polite and friendly to him?" "Yes, I am."

"And why are you so nice to him, when he is so unfriendly to you?"

"Because I don't want him to decide how I'm going to act."

INSIGHT NO 2 ...

... THE INSIDE STORY

INSIGHT NO 2

That story about John's Friend leads us also to this Insight No 2, which is 'the other side of the coin' to that first Insight No 1.

Insight No 1 tells us that what 'difficult people' say or do is out there, outside of you, it is their stuff, ... Even if they are with you, looking at you, talking to you, even talking about you, using your name, ... they are still on the outside, outside your skin.

However, how you react inside and what happens inside of you (inside your skin) is very much your stuff, ... very much your business. How you respond to, speak to and treat others speaks volumes about you, ... not them.

So, this Insight No 2 tells us that what counts is not what happens to us or around us, but what happens inside of us ... we always have a choice of how we respond.

NO ONE CAN MAKE US MAD OR SAD OR GLAD ... WITHOUT OUR PLAYING A PART IN THE DRAMA.

It is absolutely fundamental that you do not allow anybody (friend or foe) to push the buttons on your inner life, ... on your choices, your decisions or feelings.

In this sense, the task of managing 'difficult people' can really be said to be more about managing ourselves, ...

So important are Insight No 1 and Insight No 2 and that inside-outside perspective, that they make up the entire basis of the 'first step' in the book "Build Yourself a Better Life: The First Step", (to be published in Sep 2013).

> *The one thing you can't take away from me is the way I choose to respond to what you do to me ...*
>
> *The last of one's freedoms is to choose one's attitude in any given circumstance ...*
>
> *There is always a choice!*
>
> *VIKTOR FRANKL*

How a person treats you is their Karma, ...

How you react and how you treat others is yours.

As we said, the outstanding leaders, the great charismatic speakers and the top negotiators have this ability to distinguish what goes on outside from what goes on inside - not letting any negativity through to their inner thoughts or feelings.

He who drives you mad ... controls you!

Because they have mastered this inside-outside perspective, you will identify such people easily - you will hear them use "I" statements and "I" messages, expressing their preferences and their inside feelings. Other than praising, they will not use very many "You" messages ... no attacking or retaliating or putting down. Few of their sentences begin with someone else's name.

<u>With whose name do many of your sentences begin?</u>

Another question for you:

What are the consequences of you letting the 'difficult people' get to you?

When we are in a relaxed and calm state, at our best, we feel in control of ourselves and our world, … with a sense of 'can do': "I am well able for this task in hand;" "I am on top of things;" … life is good, it's a good old world.

In this state, our whole physiology is at ease, our breathing calm, … we can now deploy our talents easily, we can make best use of our thinking abilities, we are very much in control of and on top of things, we are 'in flow', we are in **our 'green zone'**.

When we choose to allow our 'difficult people' to 'rattle our cage', we quickly enter an agitated state; feelings of anger, insecurity and stress instantly replace those at-ease, 'in control', 'can do' feelings; our bodies tense up and start pumping flight-fight hormones.

Critically, our thinking quickly freezes up or looses calm perspective.

"Do not let the behaviour of others destroy your inner peace."

So, the consequence of those changes is that, in the heat of the moment, our inner emotions and thinking are 'out of control', our creativity is shut off, we can blurt out words and behave in ways, which are far beneath our normal everyday best performance.

Our agitation is evident in our body language, in our breathing and in our voice tonality, we have entered **our 'red zone'**.

To enter our 'red zone' can start a vicious circle, ... in the end, the 'difficult people' are now dictating our inner lives, ... and they are now in control of our inner lives and choices, and our performance.

"Speak when you are angry," said American Author Ambrose Bierce, "and you will make the best speech you will ever regret."

Another Story for you:

This is a brilliant and most instructive story, which I first heard from Tony Humphreys, in an excellent talk by the leading psychologist and author.

A teaching colleague at work makes a loud public comment to Dan in front of all the other teachers, asking: "Dan, do you have any control over the children in your classroom?" Dan now has the insight to know that this comment is about the speaker and, so, he calmly returns the projection to her with the question: "Mary, what makes you say that?"

Mary may respond with another "You" message, such as: "Well, you appear to let your class run riot!" Again, it is important for Dan not to react or to start defending himself or to attack back. A better strategy is to get Mary to talk about herself, rather than about him.

Dan just calmly returns the ball: "Mary, I'm wondering what it is about my class that is affecting you?" It is now possible that Mary may move towards sending an "I" message and Dan may see a beginning to her owning her own stuff.

And so the story goes, ...

Is it 'ringing any bells' for you?

Have you ever been involved in or witnessed any incidents such as this?

"Well, I found that one of your class was very impertinent, when I asked him to behave in the school-yard." Now, the playing field is a bit more level. Again, putting the responsibility back to Mary, Dan could ask: "I'm sorry to hear that. Is there something you would like me to do about what happened?"

Finally, Mary may now state the hidden but real purpose of her first "You" message. "Well, yes, I did feel a bit humiliated by the child's behaviour and I would like you to 'take him to task' about the way he carried on."

Dan now has a choice about how he might like to respond to Mary's request, ... if at all. At this point, Dan can see so clearly that Mary's original (apparently) offensive outburst was really about Mary and not really anything at all about Dan.

INSIGHT NO 3 ...

... IT TAKES TWO TO TANGO!

INSIGHT NO 3

How can you have a tennis match or a boxing match without two opponents? It takes two to tango, ...

People, who work on the frontline in a customer service role (eg complaints departments, some public offices) gain great skill at dealing with 'difficult people', ... often these Customers are in a very irate and agitated state, and are totally unreasonable. Staff quickly learn that, no matter how angry the Customer is, they will be unable to 'keep the storm raging', unless they have resistance and opposition to help them. If they are met with calm easy listening, the storm blows itself out in a minute or two, ... no more.

In fact, experienced frontline staff tell me that, very often, it is the most awkward and angry Customers who prove to be the most stressed and vulnerable internally, ... in greatest need of help!

Only 'hurt people' try to hurt people!

OF FUNDAMENTAL IMPORTANCE:

The objective of this is <u>not</u> about being quiet when you should really speak up or speak out, ... it is about never ever reacting from your 'red zone' - without you thinking!

In engagements such as in the above scenario, without any doubt, the best and most helpful strategies are calm and cool "I" messages and "I" statements, ... the use of "You" statements invariably adds fuel to that fire, ... energy to the storm.

If the situation calls for assertiveness on your part, calm "I" statements are still the most effective, ... without any need of any hint of apology, ... more on this later.

Would you believe that Business & Life Coaches now go as far as saying that it even takes someone to continue to play the victim, ... in order to allow a bully to continue to play the bully? Even in this case, it seems, it takes two to tango!

[If you are worried about bullying, or if you feel you are being bullied, please see pages 54, 55.]

INSIGHT NO 4 ...

... IS ENVY THEIR REAL DRIVER?

INSIGHT NO 4

Think for a moment about the driving force behind the aggressive attacks of these 'difficult people'. Intuitively, we can know that one likely motivation may well be just good old-fashioned envy or jealousy.

In particular, if you show a certain talent, to which they have long aspired, their reaction can be to attack, ... in an attempt to drag you down to their level.

> *Learn to re-interpret negative things that others say about you.*
>
> *See their criticisms as a cry for help, as they wish they were as amazing as you, ...*
>
> *PAUL MCKENNA*

You need to learn to re-interpret negative things that others say about you. See their criticisms as a cry for help, as they wish they were amazing, ... as you are!

"Don't let the noise of others' opinions drown out your own inner voice."

When we are at our best, we can more easily know that these 'difficult people' are also human beings, with all of the infinite possibilities and potentiality that that bestows.

For all of their unacceptable behaviours, comments and horrible taunts, they are doing the best they can at the moment, with the resources they have got at the moment. At the moment, they are struggling their very best from within the prison and internal suffering, that they have built for themselves.

"The way of the miracle worker," says Marianne Williamson, "is to see all human behaviour as one of two things - either love, ... or a call for love!"

Martin Luther King, Jr teaches us that "Darkness cannot drive out darkness, only light can do that; hate cannot drive out hate, only love can do that."

INSIGHT NO 5 ...

... IF YOU SPOT IT, ...

... HAVE YOU GOT IT?

INSIGHT NO 5

As you listen to and watch the 'difficult people' in your life, remain very aware, ... observe and learn: If you can spot it, maybe you got it ... the very feature, that annoys you most in someone else, may well be something in yourself.

Ask yourself this: What is it about you, which you see mirrored in them, which makes you so mad?

> *Everything that irritates us about others can lead us on to an understanding of ourselves, ...*
>
> **CARL JUNG**

Our feelings about ourselves can determine and be reflected in our feelings towards others. If we are ill at ease with ourselves, we can't really be at ease with others. Could it be, as Paulo Coelho might say, that our obstacles are all of our own creation, ... our freedom needs nothing more than our own declaration?

INSIGHT NO 6 ...

ANOTHER QUESTION TO YOU:

WHY DO BAD THINGS HAVE TO HAPPEN TO US AT ALL?

INSIGHT NO 6

• • • • • • • • • • • • • • • • •

Why do 'difficult people' have to come into our lives in the first place?

In order to stretch us and in order for us to grow and to learn and to have fun and to live, we need obstacles of all kinds, including the arrival of 'difficult people' into our lives.

A smooth sea never made a skilful sailor.

How else are we to grow ... except through facing into these ever more difficult challenges and obstacles?

What is life all about ... if not also about growing and learning and having fun? It may be appealing to us to lock into our comfort zone when a new obstacle comes along, to avoid it rather than to face it, ... but is this not a form of a slow boring pointless living death?

In life, our opportunities to learn are repeated, until the lesson is learned. Each lesson can be presented to us again and again in various forms, until we have learned it, … then we can move on to the next lesson.

God or Life, in wisdom or kindness, sends us these gifts to challenge us, … they are fodder for our growth; practice sessions and case studies to test us and sharpen our talents and our skills base.

So, the next time a really nasty plonker arrives into your life, say a wee "Thank you, God, … for this great gift."

> *So, he or she is really driving you nuts at the moment, …*
>
> *Hey, have you any idea who your <u>next bigger challenge</u> is likely to be?*

… and know that as you grow and up-skill to deal ever more easily with this difficult person, God and Life will help you to attract an even tougher bigger obstacle into your life, an even more difficult person, … more fodder, another test, more material for more practice, … another great gift, … just for you!

WHAT TO DO, ...

... IN THE HEAT OF THE MOMENT!

WHAT TO DO 1

Based on those six insights and on the experience of our most successful Participants, ... the best advice for coping is ... when the 'difficult people' hit on you, if you are going to stay and engage, the most critical strategy is to remember that Insight No 1: Realise immediately that what any other person believes, thinks, feels, says or does is about them, ... it's not about you, it's 100% about them.

It is just so important to develop that habit of <u>not internalising</u> what others say or do. You need to stop and you need to hear yourself asking yourself this question: "It is nothing about me: what is this saying about him or her?"

An old Zen saying teaches us that inner peace can begin the very first moment we choose not to allow an outside event or person to control our inner emotions. At first, this may be a challenge in the heat of the moment, ... but it is only difficult for the first once or twice, ... with practice, it becomes easy second nature. Read on!

There are some people who are always angry, ... always looking for conflict. Walk away, their battle is with themselves, ... it is not with you!

When the 'difficult people' hit on you, if there is any danger at all of you getting flooded or over-whelmed in the white heat of the moment, don't stay, ... disengage or get out - physically or mentally,

... or buy some time - some way, any way, ... "Excuse me, I just have to check up on something, I will be back in a moment, ..."

If you are caught in a meeting or speaking in public, buy time, ...
"Yes, I can see that you have a point, thank you, we will be coming back to that later on, ..."

When I shut my mouth and walk away, it doesn't mean you win.

It simply means that your stupid sorry show ain't worth any more of my time!

Anonymous School Girl, 15 years old.

> " *Parents of rebellious teenagers are past masters at silently biting their tongues in the reddest of 'red zone' moments, ... even if they feel like their jaws are about to explode! Yes, it is possible!*

When the 'difficult people' hit on you, ... if you are going to stay and engage, ... in the white heat of the moment, calm 'defenceless' listening, calm third-party questions, calm "I" messages, calm "I" statements are your best tactic, all the while remaining firmly in your 'green zone', ... if at all possible, quietly and calmly put the ball right back into their court - just like Dan in our story on pages 25, 26.

Responses such as these are most unhelpful: "You really cannot be serious;" "No, that will never work;" "That's a crazy proposal;" "You must be joking;" "You can't be seriously suggesting that." These just open the door to a duel of egos, a see-saw contest of relative personal worth to no one's benefit. Disaster!

It is much better to push the issue and the focus away from them and away from yourself, using third-party questions; this can avoid the confrontational see-saw duel of personalities: "What worries would you think our CEO (not You, not I) might have about the costs involved in your proposal?"

Every challenge in life can make us or break us; every difficulty can make us either bitter or bigger and better; the choice is always ours … to be the victim or the victor.

"You either step forward into growth or step back into safety", says Abraham Maslow.

So, explore every incident, … in order to learn!

Or "How do you think the financial figures of your proposal will stand up to the scrutiny of our Finance Team?" "How sure can we be that our Customers will understand such a new offering so quickly?" "Maybe our Team might find it easier to explore such a total work change - step by step, … one step at a time."

When all is said and done, unfortunately, you cannot count on others to treat you with respect - treating others with respect does not guarantee that you will be treated with respect by them. In the final analysis, you have control only over yourself, your behaviour, how you choose to be as a person, how you respond to the 'difficult people'. As for others, you cannot forcibly change them. In the final analysis, you can only accept them, or influence them to see some light … or walk away.

Move along to bigger and better things. Forgive and forget, … not because they deserve it, but because you do!

In one coaching workshop, Michael, a 'drive-ahead' small business owner, complained: "Yes, I heard you say that managing the 'difficult people' is really about managing myself, ... but my expectation coming here was that you would equip me with verbal tricks and smarter lines, ... so that I could really defeat my opponents into submission, making them look really bad in front of everyone," ... Wrong, Michael, wrong!

Numerous surveys on leadership traits have been identifying emotional stability as the No 1 attribute, which most people seek out in both business and political leaders. When 'all hell breaks loose', people value and admire those who remain calm and thinking, in full control of their emotions and do not become rattled or lose their temper or loose perspective in their thinking.

In stark contrast, a high and permanent price is paid for angry outbursts or 'out of control' rants. People are pushed away <u>not</u> won by emotional in-stability. Impatient outbursts from your 'red zone' can do permanent damage - to you! Don't make the greatest speech that you will ever regret. You are much too good for all of that - never, ever risk it!

You win by remaining calm in the face of the intense provocation. You prove that you are above the 'difficult people', bigger than the present situation, better than it all!

WHAT TO DO, ...

... PREPARING IN ADVANCE!

WHAT TO DO 2

It is really a very poor strategy to just sit and hope that the 'difficult people' in your life will go away or that they will suddenly have a miraculous change of attitude and start totally leaving you alone.

It is best to be proactive: review your current scenario; prepare and plan in advance; ... then practise, practise, practise, ... To help you to do that, here are three exercises devised for our coaching workshops. Please do not just read through them or do them 'in your head'; do get out your pencil and some blank sheets of paper, ... I promise you that you will be truly amazed at the outcome!

> *It is best to treat all our critical relationships as re-negotiable all the time, ...*
>
> **Dr Phil McGraw**

At the very least, these exercises will put you into a mind-set to pro-actively manage your difficult relationships, rather than play victim.

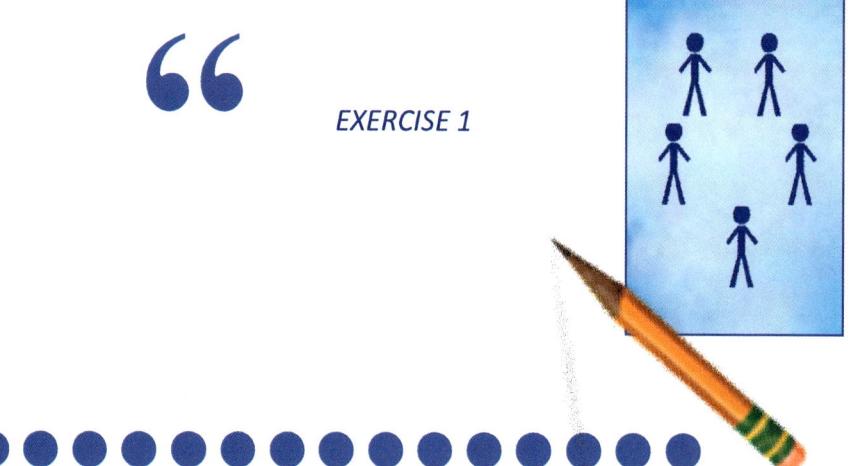

EXERCISE 1

Take that blank sheet of paper, draw five pencil people and write a name opposite each - naming the next five most 'difficult people', with whom you will have to contend. Of course, you know exactly who they are, ... they are most probably the same as the last five!

Now, one by one, in respect of each of these five, can you recount or get a sense of your inner talk sequences, when you last encountered them? What were you saying to yourself inside? What were you thinking? What were you feeling inside?

When are you likely to next meet them? Where? Can you close your eyes and visualise yourself dealing in a calm and cool style with their put downs and horrible taunts? What would you like to be thinking now? What are you saying now? How are you saying it?

Can you see yourself, ... your coolness; your posture; your easy, relaxed, re-assured breathing and you calm voice tonality?

AND PRACTISE, …

PRACTISE, …

PRACTISE, …

Alone, in a quiet safe place, … predict what the 'difficult people' will be saying in that next incident, … then, visualise and actually stand up, your shoulders back, in a calm, assertive state, … just as you will stand. And as you stand tall there now, allow your whole physiology to fill out to its full height, allow your posture to 'say it all'! Every cell of your body will be eavesdropping on your new thinking, … re-enforcing that calm new You. Be ready to fake it, until you make it!

Practise your calm words aloud again and again. Practise the "I" statements you will use, if you choose to say out what it is you would prefer, specifying these clearly and calmly, without apology: "Tom, actually, I am not comfortable when you joke like that." "To be honest, Joan, I find those comments unacceptable." "Chris, this Team is way too successful for that kind of negative sarcasm."

At first, it may take an opportunity or two for you to remain fully calm in the face of their verbal attacks. Continue to practise, practise, practise. Your new life and new freedom will be worth it.

"

EXERCISE 2

The eraser says it all, …

Is it time you de-cluttered your life of the negative people around you? Is it time that you re-claimed back your freedom, your fun and your life?

Maybe you don't need to manage the 'difficult people' in your life, so much as you need to start moving in different and better circles, … surrounding yourself with positive people, who support you and re-enforce your positive self image. Maybe we can simply change the people we choose to be around, … rather than trying in vain to change the people around us!

What about a deliberate effort to list down, seek out and sail with better friends and company, giving your list of negative friends a very wide berth, … seeking out confidantes and friends, who will always put you up, … never drag you down?

EXERCISE 3

Would you like to carry out a quick but accurate ten-minute audit of your life and how you are doing, ... right at the moment? OK?

Again, take a blank sheet of paper and, again, draw five pencil people, writing a name opposite each, ... this time, write the names of the five people with whom you spend most of your time at the moment. No, not who you like best, nor who you enjoy most, nor who you would like to spend most time with, ... Who do you actually spend most time with, ... these days?

How happy are these five? How much fun do they have? What is their level of achievement to date? How successful are they now? What is their level of income? How positive are they? Are they really going places?

Are you ok with all of that? Is it possible you have outgrown them as friends?

BIRDS OF A FEATHER, ...

... THEY ALWAYS FLOCK TOGETHER!

Many newly-trained Business & Life Coaches say that the five people, with whom you spend most time, present a very accurate reflection of how you yourself are doing, right now. In short hand, you will hear them say: "You are the sum total of these five people." "Birds of a feather, they always flock together," they say.

Did you proactively choose those friends, or did happen-chance or fate or accident select them? Is it time you re-visited some or all of those decisions?

On the other hand, let us remember, as Mother Teresa taught us, "some people come into our lives as blessings, some come as lessons." How long has it been since you used your pencil to list your blessings? Maybe it is again time for you to list and to seek out your "real" friends, ... and to enjoy spending much more time with them!

JUST GO DO IT!

ENJOY, ...

AND HAVE WONDERFUL FUN!

Very many Participants in our coaching workshops seem to think that Business & Life Coaches themselves were surely born with all of those insights and skills. I can tell you, with absolute certainty, that nothing could be further from the truth, ...

You can always know the blacksmith's pony by his lame step.

I myself learned the insights and lessons in this book so very, very slowly. Maybe, it's the lessons, which we need most, that we learn most slowly ... but, maybe, we learn those lessons best!

To be honest, my own experience was that, for years and years, I stubbornly refused to hear anything of those six insights, ... nobody but nobody could get through to me. This meant so much time in my 'red zone', ... damaging my career and my business and adding fuel to quite high stress levels.

One new insight can change you instantly and permanently, ... but only when you are ready to let it in, ...

Don't leave it so long, ... as I did!

Eventually, after many years, I somehow suddenly let some light in, ... I let those insights get through to me. Very strangely, without great difficulty, I then immediately began to visualise, to practise, practise, practise and to implement the skills and new approach!

To be honest, I was so very happy and ready to fake it all, until I could make it all!

My ability and my style at managing my 'difficult people' soared sharply. As soon as the insights got through to me, the new skills came really quickly, ... almost overnight. From that moment on, their 'jibes' and 'taunts' ran off me like water off a duck! Their 'put downs' not longer impacted me!

As you can imagine, my career and my business improved rapidly, my stress levels quickly faded away ... I was an instant overnight success after so many years of floundering!

"

Major personal change can be slow, tedious and very hard work!

But it can also be fun, effortless, instant yet permanent, ...

... if you choose it to be that way!

In fact, I believe that dramatic personal change mostly happens in an instant, ... when we gain that new insight or experience ... in a split second. Can you remember your last major personal change? How quick was it?

I hope you give yourself the time to engage fully with the questions and the exercises in this book and that you will also let those six insights through to you, ... without the years and years of floundering that I brought upon myself! I certainly wish for you the same effortless and fun transformation, which I eventually enjoyed.

Just go do it, enjoy it, ... stay curious and exploring, and have wonderful fun with it all!

Thank you very much for downloading and reading this book. I wish You the very, very best in all things, J Rochie Holohan.

You are invited to read …

OTHER BOOKS TO BE PUBLISHED

by J ROCHIE HOLOHAN

You are particularly invited to read Rochie's next book "Build Yourself a Better Life: The First Step" (to be published in Sep 2013). The insights and personal changes recommended here in this 'Difficult People' book are based directly on those suggested in that 'First Step' book.

Also, Rochie is working on nine further books, all based on the issues he regularly presents and discusses in those coaching workshops:

> *How to Manage the Problem Employee;*
> *How to Manage Personal Stress;*
> *How to Beat Procrastination;*
> *Executive Time Management Skills;*
> *Concentration, Study & Exam Skills;*
> *CV Preparation & Interviewee Skills;*
> *Executive Leadership Skills;*
> *Charisma & Public Speaking Skills;*
> *Build Yourself a Better Life: The Final Steps.*

Having studied for many years with the renowned Professor Roger Bennett at the IMCB in Buckingham in England, Rochie graduated with a Masters Degree in Management Training.

Later, his research work in training was rewarded with a Fellowship of the UK Chartered Institute of Personnel Development and a Fellowship of the Irish Institute of Training and Development.

Rochie thanks Colin Brett, Philip Brew and the Tipperary Institute in Thurles in County Tipperary in Ireland for qualifications as a Life & Business Coach.

Rochie has Practitioner Certificates in (NLP) Neuro Linguistic Programming, (TLT) Time Line Therapy and Hypnosis. In 2007, he got Master Practitioner Certificates in these three disciplines.

About your Coach ...

J ROCHIE HOLOHAN FCIPD FIITD

As well as his work in Ireland, Northern Ireland and England, Rochie works as a senior consultant in Denmark, Eastern Europe, Russia, the Seychelles Islands and Zambia. Those projects are mainly about strengthening critical organisations, through the training and coaching of Senior Managers and the training of Trainers.

Rochie worked for many years with a number of local county councils in Ireland and as the chief executive of a local not-for-profit enterprise promotion company. Since Oct 2009, Rochie has been running his own coaching and training business from his spiritual home on the most westerly corner of Europe, from the wild and beautiful West Kerry.

He now leads open and in-company coaching workshops at home and abroad, ... focused mainly on leadership, supervision, strategy, stress management, public speaking skills or training-of-trainers.

❝❝

LEGAL NOTICE : DISCLAIMER

This book is provided "as is" without warranty of any kind, either expressed or implied. The Publisher or the Author make no representations with respect to the contents of this work. You are cautioned to rely on your own judgment about your own individual circumstances and to act accordingly.

This book is certainly not intended as a substitute for professional psychotherapy. Nor is it intended for use as a source of accounting, business, financial, legal or medical advice. All readers are advised to seek the services of competent professionals in all such matters.

In particular, it is your own responsibility to keep yourself safe and free from harm. If you do not feel well and safe, please contact your own public or private medical service immediately or your national emergency phone number.

KEEPING YOURSELF SAFE

If you feel vulnerable or afraid, or if you are being bullied or subjected to abusive treatment, … and you feel that you may not be able to cope, be sure to also reach out to a friend or a family member.

Or, … do make immediate contact with your medical professional or with one of the many support organisations in your region, … that's what they are there for, that's what they have been trained to do and that's what they do, … day in and day out!

Yes, life can be and usually is a bit of an up-and-down journey. We all have our down times and our up times. Is it not time we took the support that's there for us? How long do you think it will be, … before it is time for you or me to lend that same support to other friends?

ACKNOWLEDGEMENTS ...

*"If I have seen a little further,
it is only by standing on
the shoulders of giants,"
Isaac Newton, 1676.*

All Rochie's books are based on the work of the world's leading authors on personal achievement and leadership, including John Adair, Richard Bandler, Warren Bennis, Stephen R Covey, Peter Drucker, John Grinder, Viktor Frankl, Charles Handy, John Humble, Tony Humphreys, Antony Jay, John Kotter, Alan Lakein, Charles Margerison, Abraham Maslow, Dick McCann, Paul McKenna, Henry Mintzberg, Charles Perrow, Tom Peters, Derek Pugh, Anthony Robbins, Brian Tracy and Ken Wydro.

So much thanks is also due to Cedric Chau, Eamon Murray, Edmond Holohan, Emer Howard, Garrett Fitzgerald, John J Sheahan, Lena Holohan, Máire Uí Léime and Patrick Casey.

Obviously, the books also owe a major amount to the Participants of our coaching workshops, who contributed so honestly and openly to the many conversations, which led directly to the contents of these books. In fact, for the most part, these materials first saw 'light of day' as ms powerpoint slides in those coaching workshops.

66

YOUR COMMENTS ARE INVITED ...

WE WOULD LOVE TO HEAR FROM YOU!

Unlike traditional books, for better or worse, 'Createspace' books can now be updated. For that reason, any comments or suggestions you may have would be most welcome. Simply e-mail Rochie (with the name of the book in the subject line) to jrochieholohan@iol.ie.

As we said, all of the ideas in this book were presented and discussed with the Participants in our coaching workshops, many of whom already had extensive successful experience in business and life. Indeed, all the ideas benefit from the long hours of sharing of (good and bad) experiences, of frank scrutiny and of exploratory discussions.

So, you can see why Rochie so welcomes any comments, new stories or new suggestions. Yes, we would love to hear from you, ...

Published by

CREATESPACE.COM

Author

J Rochie Holohan,
Coast Guard Cottages,
Ballydavid,
County Kerry,
Ireland.

jrochieholohan@iol.ie

www.jrochieholohan.com

ISBN - 10: 1482025086
ISBN - 13: 9781482025088